S0-BIN-286

Our Place DARIEN™

Written by
Chris Gorman and Michelle Morfitt

Published by

HOMETOWN 520 LLC

Hometown 520, LLC
Rowayton, CT 06853
www.ourplacebooks.com

Printed on 100% recycled paper in the USA
ISBN: 978-0-9822205-1-1

While Jack is a smart and very well read golden retriever, the facts found in this book are to the best of his (and the authors) knowledge at the time of printing.

Special thanks to all those who submitted artwork for the cover

Uday Avula
Marissa Baker
Britton Barthold
Aislinn Bevill
Ben Boston
PK Brannigan
Ricahard Brereton
Charlie Brooks
Daphne Budd
Roisin Burke
Charlotte Byrne
Dh Cahoon
Ashley Cassetta
Morgan Cockrell
Will Collier
Ben Collier
Patricia Collins
Emily Conn
Aidan Coyle
Emily Coyle
James Crafford
Charlie Craigin
Katherine Culliton
Charlie Dean
Brandon Delgatto
Breana Delgatto
Lucas Fee
Gianni Filippone
Jane Firmin
Jack Flanagan
Robbie Foresta
Tina Glekas
Murphy Grady
Dolan Gregorich
Sarah Hadlow
Natalie Hartokolis
Jack Henrich
Samira Huerlimann
Emma Hunter
Isa Johnston
Morgan Kennedy
Lindsay Kirby
Tommy Kyritz
Haley Laughlin
Claire Lincoln*
Christine Matyszkowicz
Sabrina Mcdonnell
Ashley Mclaren
Matthew Medwid
Colin Minicus
Kristen Moran
Abbie Mueller
Riley Mullin
Kate Nusslein
Cary O'Brien
Katie O'Connor
Jimmy Odell
Christian Osterberg
Michael Parsley
Jack Payne
Giselle Perkowski
Laura Pizzani
Billy Platt
Claire Plunkett
Jenni Previte
Allen Reed
Peter Ridder
JP Roach
Sarah Roney
Susie Ropp
Bella Sapio
Matt Sealy
Paige Sommer
Brian Stute
Jack Thornbury
Caroline Tortorella
Hannah Vogel
Jack Wells
Finley Wetmore
Charlie Wolf
Helen Wolf

*Winner

FOREWORD

It was with nervous anticipation that I arrived at the central offices of the Darien Public Schools in July of 2005. I was excited and proud to have been accepted by the Board of Education as the new Assistant Superintendent for Elementary Education. After 30 plus years as a teacher and administrator in New York State, I was heading into new territory, Fairfield County, Connecticut. As a newcomer to Darien, a read through Our Place, Darien would have been a blessing, giving me a panoramic view of key sites in this delightful community as well as an historical perspective on its growth and development.

Right from the title, Our Place, Darien hints of the warm and friendly literacy trip parents can take with their children through the town of Darien with all its historical culture and physical charm. Through the inquisitive eyes of Jack, a bright and frisky golden retriever, you can travel through Darien viewing delicate, pastel illustrations of the many features that make it a unique Connecticut community.

While reading Our Place, Darien, I could imagine authors Michelle Morfitt and Chris Gorman snuggled on a couch sharing the book with their three children. They know their children will enjoy following Jack as he points out special places in Darien like the Nature Center, the Darien Playhouse, and the waterfront, often from different vantage points. They anticipate their children's reactions when they learn that Siwanoy Indians were the original inhabitants and that the name of Darien was borrowed from the Isthmus of Darien in Panama. But more than that, Michelle and Chris await those sections of Our Place, Darien that encourage their children to appreciate the delicate shoreline environment of Darien and to protect its exceptional flora and fauna.

Authors, Michelle Morfitt and Chris Gorman, have crafted a unique literary experience with their Our Place series of books. What a pleasant introduction to Darien it will be for families new to the area to walk through the town with Jack as their guide. Families that have been in Darien for generations will also enjoy reading this lovely depiction of their community and might learn some new information as well. Perhaps they could add some unique tales of their own.

As a lifelong teacher, I can envision Our Place, Darien and its companion books as valuable literary additions to any classroom. What a wonderful way for the children of Darien to learn about their community. There are so many connections that teachers can make to the study of history, culture, and the environment. The Our Place series can stimulate the thinking of even the youngest students about the characteristics that make each town unique and about the perspectives that youngsters develop as they grow up in a particular place. The possibilities are endless.

It is a great pleasure for me to welcome you to read Our Place, Darien. I warn you that you'll want to read it again and again to absorb all it has to offer about our town Darien. You'll want to visit places that you didn't know existed or search for Darien's particular breed of plants and animals. You might even decide to grow an organic garden. Enjoy the experience!

Dr. Judith Pandolfo
Assistant Superintendent Elementary Education

Hello, my name is Jack. I'm a golden retriever.

I live in the coastal town of Darien, Connecticut. Follow me, I'll tell you a bit about "Our Place."

I share my town with: 20,000 friendly humans, 5,000 other dogs, gaggles of geese, countless gulls, cormorants and sandpipers, fleeting white-tailed deer, the occasional wild turkey, squirrels, skunks, raccoons, and... rumor has it, there may be cougars, but I have yet to see one.

From the eye of a seagull, Darien looks like this.

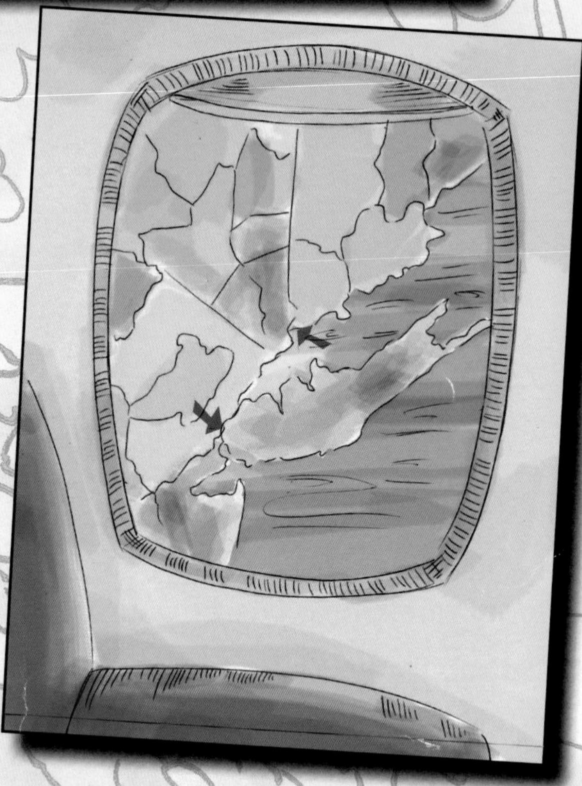

This is what Darien looks like from the window of an airplane landing at JFK airport near New York City.

This is what it looks like from the deck of a boat on the Long Island Sound.

This is what Darien looks like from the window of a train going from Grand Central Station in New York City, to South Station in Boston.

And ...driving on I-95 North.

And...this is how
it looks to a truck
trying to take
a short cut through
our town.

It is likely that meat eating dinosaurs lived not too far from Darien. Dilophosaurus tracks were found near here that measured 10-16 inches long and 3 to 4 feet apart. Dilophosaurus lived during the early Jurassic period, some 200 million years ago.

The first people to live in Darien were the Siwanoy Indians. They were peaceful, nomadic people, which means, they preferred to wander about the countryside, sleeping and eating as they chose.

In 1640, the English settlers came to Darien.

The newcomers were welcomed to the area by Siwanoy Chief Piamikin, who agreed to sell the land to the new white men, in exchange for one hundred bushels of corn, four coats and some tobacco.

The Siwanoy tribe lived peacefully alongside the new settlers for a while, but then chose to drift off on their nomadic way, to find more space to roam.

For over a hundred years our town became known as Middlesex Parish.

In the early 1800s, the population of Middlesex Parish had grown to over 1,000 people, who decided to incorporate as a town.

Thaddeus Bell was Darien's first citizen. He was responsible for the town's independence from Stamford and Norwalk. His friends suggested the town be named 'Bellville' but he humbly declined.

In 1820, our town was named Darien. The name Darien was suggested by Bell after speaking with Captain Isaac Weed, a local sailor who had recently visited the Isthmus of Darien, in Panama.

In 1969, a mayor from the State of Illinois visited Connecticut. He liked our town so much that he decided to name his own town in Illinois 'Darien.'

Our town transforms itself four times a year with the wonderful seasons. My favorite season is spring where I feel a little extra bounce in my paws.

Cherry Lawn Park is one of my favorite hangouts. There are lots of guys to play with, and lots of moms I like to fetch the ball for.

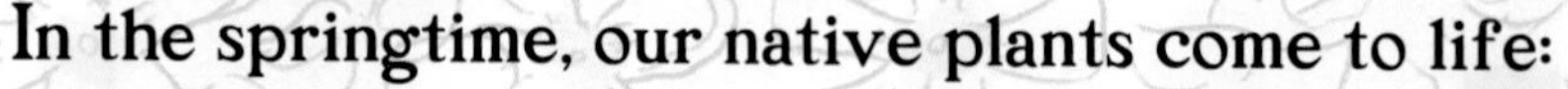

In the springtime, our native plants come to life:

These are rhododendrons

These are daffodils

These are snowdrops

This is creeping phlox

In the late 1600s, the new settlers cut roads through the thick woods in Darien. Their main country road went through Middlesex Parish and became known as "Old Kings Highway." Judy Groppa told me that in 1807, the Post Road was opened and a daily mail service was established.

The Stamford Street Railroad Co. provided a trolley service to downtown Darien and the Post Road became the perfect place for stores to display their wares. The shops along the Post Road sold hats, shoes and other sundries.

We no longer share our downtown streets
with trolley cars and mailmen on horseback,
but some very large strollers.

In spring, music fills the air when our native birds return, singing as they tend to their nests and lay their eggs.

The beautiful birds which roost in our town include:

Egrets

Red winged blackbirds

Ruby throated hummingbirds

Red cardinals

Blue jays

Speaking of flying, Charles Lindbergh is a famous pilot who lived on Tokeneke Trail Road in Darien. He was the first pilot to fly all by himself from New York to Paris, France in 1927.

Darien gets almost 4 feet of rain a year – most of it falls during springtime. All Darien residents are lucky enough to have clean drinking water available year round from faucets inside their homes. The town's water is stored in 3 towers containing a total of 2.75 million gallons. The tower on Mansfield Avenue was built in 1937.

Spring is the best time of year to collect rain water to water the garden.

And the best time to plant organic vegetables.

At the end of spring, the whole town celebrates Memorial Day, remembering the brave humans who fought for our country. There is a parade featuring proud members of today's community.

In 1864, Darien became the home for all the disabled veterans and orphans of soldiers in the Civil War. The generous Darienite, Benjamin Fitch, founded and funded the home. It was the first of its kind in the United States.

SUMMERTIME
in Darien is wonderful.
We are surrounded by the Long Island Sound, which comes alive with activity. We goldens love the water. That's good, because more than 13% of Darien is water!
Kieran Cavanna, a local fisherman, tells me the Sound is swimming with:
Striped Bass
Porgy
Clams
Oysters

The Darien waterways flow into the Long Island Sound, an estuary, which means it is a mix of freshwater and saltwater. The freshwater comes from the Connecticut River, the Housatonic-Naugatuck River and the Shetucket-Thames River. The salt water flows from the Atlantic.

The Sound, being an estuary, is actually one of the richest breeding areas on Earth.

In the late 1700s, the Darien waterways looked much different than they do today. Sailing vessels from as far as the West Indies would dock at Gorhams' Landing and trade with the local Middlesex merchants.

Marine animals that live along our coastline must be able to handle water temperature differences from 32 degrees in the winter to 75 degrees in the summer.

The Sound is 110 miles long
and 21 miles wide at its widest point.

It is an average of 65 feet deep but
is 350 feet deep at the deepest point.
That's the height of about
10 telephone poles stacked on
top of one another!!

There are two large
streams, which flow through
the town, the Goodwives River and the
Noroton River. My friends and I enjoy swimming
in Cherry Lawn Pond, Tilley Pond and Holly Pond.

Darien is in the state of Connecticut. The name Connecticut
comes from the Mohegan Indian word Quinnehtukqut, which means
"Long River Place" or "Beside the Long Tidal River."

There are so many things to enjoy today in Darien.

We have:
2 public beaches

Pear Tree Point Beach Park and Weed Beach are available to Darienite humans, for free, all year round. Weed Beach is almost 23 acres—that is as big as 17 football fields!

Darien also has:
a movie theatre

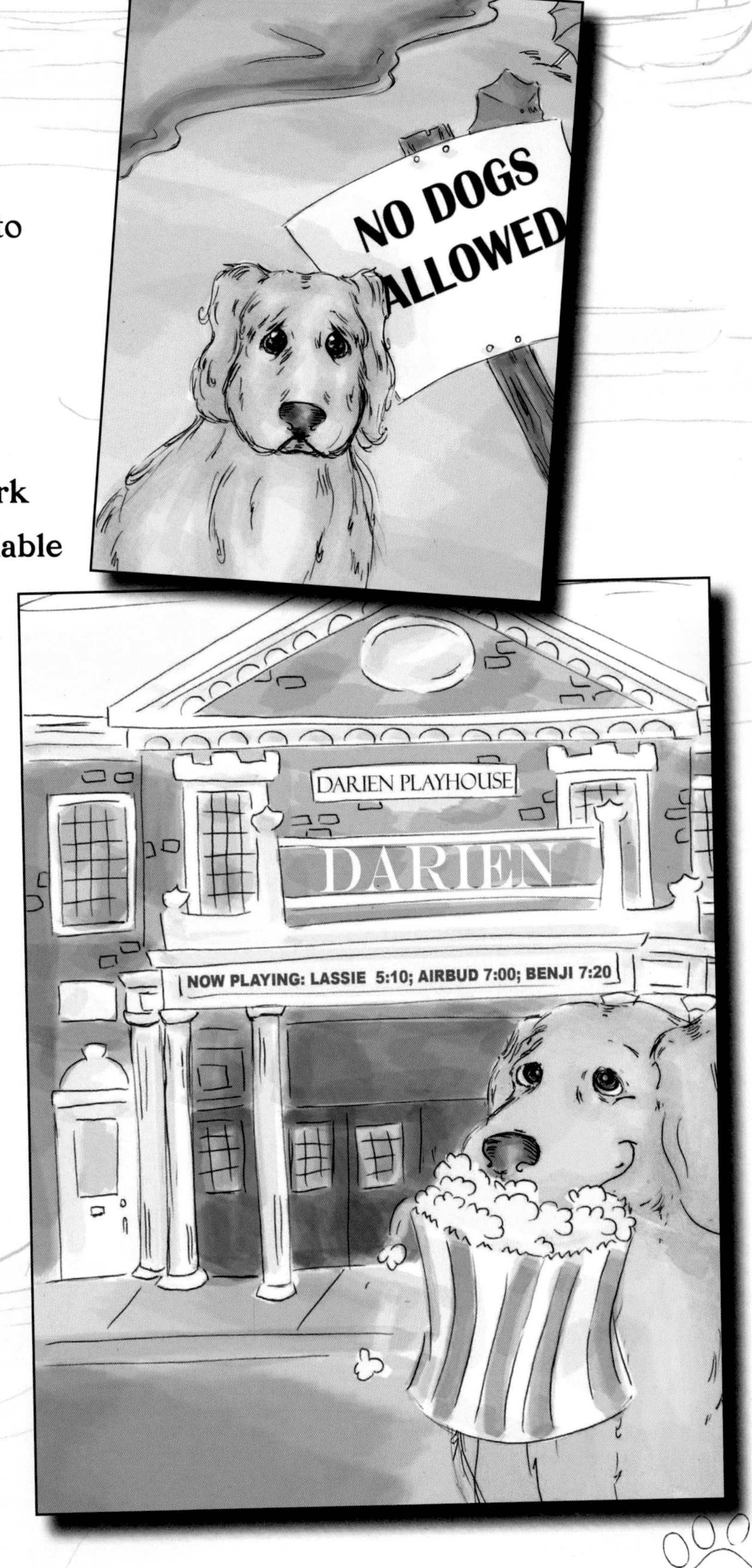

A huge public library

2 town newspapers

An ice skating rink

Darien has so many public parks and playgrounds that my paws are spoiled for choice.

Cherry Lawn Park covers 27 acres and is home to a number of my furry friends at the Darien Nature Center. They are looked after by Marie Bryan, Lynn Hamlen and other wonderful humans.

Darien continues to bloom throughout the summer

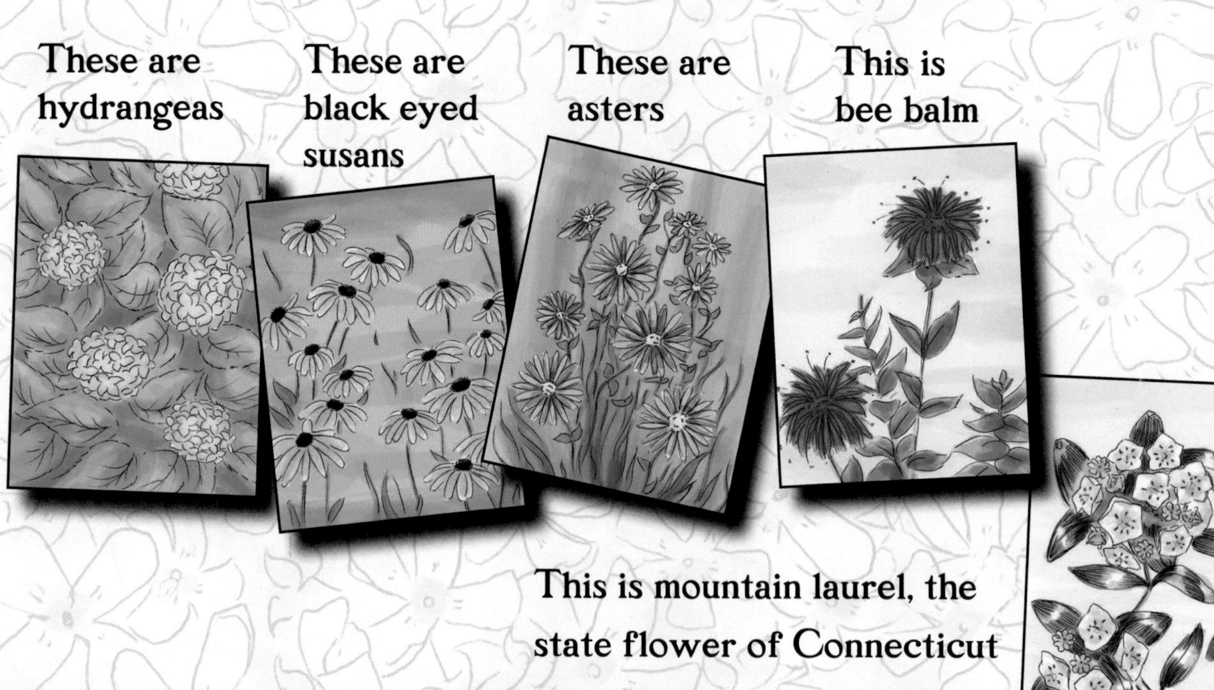

These are hydrangeas

These are black eyed susans

These are asters

This is bee balm

This is mountain laurel, the state flower of Connecticut

There is a wonderful garden at Cherry Lawn Park where Darienites grow sunflowers, pumpkins, tomatoes, squash and lots of other healthy vegetables...everything they need, except bones for me.

Alternatively, we can buy our food from:

The Farmers Market, Palmers Market, or one of the local eateries: Vavala's Deli, The Sugar Bowl, Uncle's or Post Corner Pizza.

mans in our
ike to play with
balls almost as much as
I do.

I watch them hitting them with racquets, bouncing and dunking them in nets, kicking them with their feet, and smacking them with bats.

The name "Blue Wave" was said to be coined by the great Darien football coach John Maher in 1945. He wanted to see his players tackle opponents and overcome them like a "big blue wave."

Every 4th of July,
the humans celebrate
"Independence Day,"
which is a national holiday
commemorating the end of
the American Revolution.
The U.S. broke away from
British sovereign rule on
July 4th, 1776.

At the start of the
American Revolution,
General George Washington
and 19,000 of his men
marched through Darien
on their way from Boston
to New York City.

The fall season comes as the weather starts to cool down, the foliage colors change, flowers die off, leaves on deciduous trees begin to fall, and our insect friends depart.

The leaves change color because the days get shorter and there is less sunlight.

A wise old owl in Tilley Pond Park once told me that the veins inside the leaf that carry fluids in and out, slowly close off as a layer of cells form at the bottom of each leaf. These clogged veins trap sugars in the leaf, which create color. Once the connecting tissues are sealed off, the leaf is ready to fall.

I bark goodbye to some of my bird friends who fly away to warmer climates, and welcome the new birds who like to visit and share our place during the winter months. This is called migration. Some Darien humans "migrate" to Florida during the winter too.

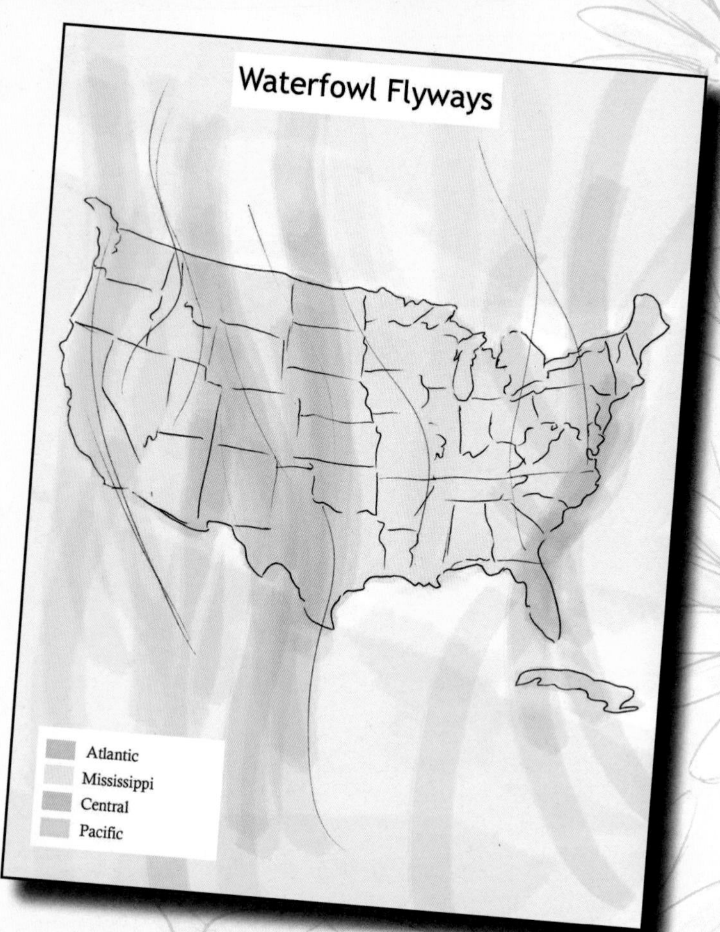

Canadian geese enjoy a stop in Darien as they travel the "Atlantic Flyway," all the way down to Florida. The Atlantic Flyway is used because no mountains or hills block the birds' path, and good sources of water and food cover the entire length.

A lot of my turkey friends must migrate too, because they always seem to go into hiding during this time of year. I think it has something to do with the humans celebrating the Thanksgiving holiday, where they pay tribute to their family and friends, and show gratitude for the food we all enjoy throughout the year here in Darien.

Roughly once every 105 dog years, that's 15 human years, we will experience a hurricane with winds of over 75 miles per hour.

These powerful storms make it impossible for me to walk down Middlesex Road. Also, trees have a hard time standing up straight and fish find themselves swimming in waterways which were not there before.

In 1938, a hurricane called "The New England Express" took Darien by surprise and caused a lot of damage. My friend Allie Rausch assures me that nowadays, safety procedures and warning systems are in place so we can be prepared if a major storm is coming, and avoid getting our paws wet.

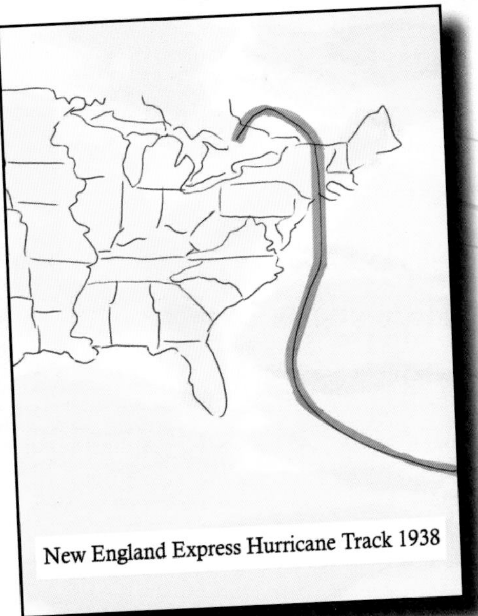

New England Express Hurricane Track 1938

The winter bears down hard as the landscape is cleansed of its vegetation, boats and pedestrians.

The land freezes, snow arrives, and most animals hibernate. Hibernation is when an animal stores enough food energy in his body, and sleeps for the whole winter. Most animals in Darien partially hibernate, sleeping for weeks, but then come out to say hello briefly on warmer days.

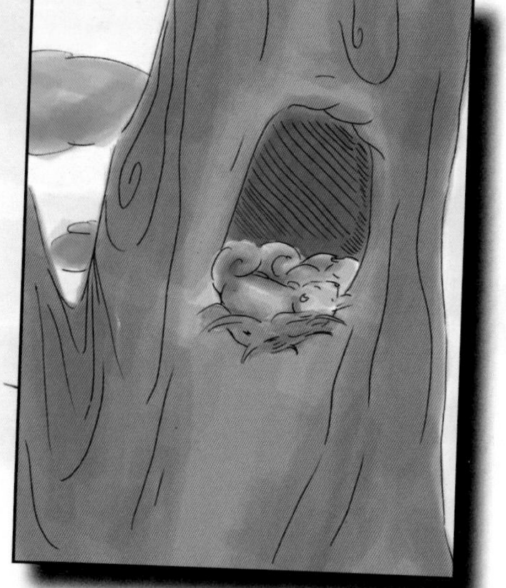

Wood burning fireplaces keep our families warm and their smoke rises up from chimneys, giving the air a distinct, wintry smell.

Darien is very lucky to be protected by 3 Volunteer Fire Departments. The Darien firefighters are always there to lend a hand and save lives.

My buddies and I are very appreciative to the 505 fire hydrants in the town.

A lot of the Darien humans celebrate the winter holidays by decorating their homes with pretty wreaths, colorful lights, giving out holiday gifts and singing carols.

Darien has had a post office in Noroton Heights since the mid 1800s. There is a lot of activity here during the winter season.

The Darien train station opened in 1848.

The human population of Darien began to increase in the late 1800s. The new train service brought people up from New York City who began to build summer homes here.

The area of Tokeneke became a popular retreat for many, including steel industry titan Andrew Carnegie. The name Tokeneke comes from one of the Indian Chiefs of the Siwanoy tribe.

I guess the visitors liked our town so much that a lot of them chose to make it their home. This was the start of Darien becoming the commuter town it remains today.

Darien has the only ambulance service in the United States that is manned by high school students. It is called Post 53 and was begun in 1970 by a great man named 'Bud' Doble.

Darien is also proud of Troop 53, the town's original Boy Scout Troop dating all the way back to 1918.

Connecticut lies on a winter storm track, influenced by the warm Gulf Stream. So, as the weather gets colder, we experience enormous winter storms called Nor' Easters', which can deposit substantial amounts of snow to play in.

My Great, great, great, great, golden grandfather told me about the Nor'easter of 1888 that started just after midnight on March 12th and dumped 50 inches of snow on Darien in one day.

That's enough snow to cover me, and my friends Calvin, Cassidy and Isla.

We usually enjoy 2 to 3 feet of snow in Darien each winter. Sadly, global warming means that the average temperature of our planet is increasing, and we will not be getting as much snow as our ancestors enjoyed.

If we all work to reduce our carbon paw print and slow climate change, we will be able to make our snowmen last longer.

This is the oldest house in Darien. It was built in 1696.

This is the greenest, most energy efficient house in Darien.

This is my house
in Darien.

Be good to each other,
love your four legged and feathered friends,
and please come and visit
"Our Place" again soon.